I HATE® KANSAS
303 Reasons Why You Should, Too

Crane Hill
PUBLISHERS
BIRMINGHAM, ALABAMA

I HATE KANSAS

303 Reasons Why You Should, Too

Paul Finebaum

CRANE HILL
PUBLISHERS

Library of Congress Cataloging-in-Publication Data

Finebaum, Paul, 1955-
  I hate Kansas: 303 reasons why you should, too / Paul Finebaum.
    p.   cm.
  ISBN 1-57587-121-1
  1. University of Kansas — Football — Miscellanea. I. Title.
GV958.U5266F55   1996
796.332'64'0978165--dc20   96-10695
                                                               CIP

10   9   8   7   6   5   4   3   2   1

I HATE KANSAS

I Hate Kansas Because…

1. Wilt Chamberlain began working on his off-court scoring record while he was a Jayhawk.

2. Like March winds and melting snow, a sure sign of spring is coach Roy Williams's new speech explaining why the Kansas Jayhawks got knocked out of the NCAA tournament.

3. The Rock Chalk Chant is the closest thing to literature to ever come out of KU.

4. Because all the pretty girls on the University of Kansas campus are just visiting.

5. One of the most popular courses for Jayhawks players is "Philosophy: Why Don't They Spell It with an 'F'?"

6. Many famous coaches have come from Kansas, but few have stayed.

7. Coach Roy Williams utterly confuses his players with his strange tic-tac-toe—they don't understand how there can be so many Xs and Os.

8. The difference between Jayhawk football and a dollar bill is that a dollar bill is good for 4 quarters.

9. Many famous coaches have come from Kansas, but none will admit it.

10. The definition of gross ignorance is 144 Jayhawks.

11. A Jayhawk with half a brain is considered gifted.

12. The easiest way to get a University of Kansas graduate off your porch is to pay him for the pizza.

13. Whenever people talk about Jayhawk basketball, they're always talking about the past.

14. Of course, with Roy Williams in the present, they don't have much of a choice.

15. At Kansas, students can actually major in "Therapeutic Recreation."

16. The top 10 ways you know you're at a Jayhawks football game: Quarterback has a flask in his back pocket.

17. Two players arrive wearing Domino's Pizza uniforms.

18. The team mascot relieves himself in the middle of the field.

19. You witness the field-goal kicker accepting cash from another man in the stadium restroom.

20. A cheerleader is breast-feeding a child between plays.

21. The coach is selling beer in the stands during halftime.

22. The running back is escorted on and off the field by state troopers.

23. The players stop during play to participate in the wave.

24. When a player comes off the field, he gives his shoes to the player going on the field.

25. It's the middle of the second quarter and the stands are already beginning to empty!

26. How many KU students does it take to change a lightbulb? Only 1, but he gets 6 hours of credit for it.

27. KU's business school offers a course in "Counterfeiting the Xerox Way."

28. Several bars in Lawrence have instituted a new rule forbidding KU cheerleaders from opening bottles with their teeth.

29. KU graduates place their diplomas in their rear windows so they'll qualify for handicapped parking.

30. The science department at KU has solar panels aimed at the moon.

31. The Jayhawk baseball team's infield chatter consists mainly of shouting, "Hit it to one of the other guys–I've got bad hands!"

32. The water fountains at KU sorority houses dispense Evian.

33. When the Jayhawk basketball team was asked to name its top role model, the players unanimously chose Dennis Rodman.

34. Coach Terry Allen often reminds his players, "Practice starts when the little hand is on the 4 and the big hand is on the 12."

35. But he had to change the policy when players with digital clocks didn't show up.

36. Wilt Chamberlain's top 10 favorite pastimes while he was a student at Kansas were: Playing basketball.

37. Playing with women.

38. Dunking the basketball.

39. Dunking women.

40. Diving for loose balls.

41. Diving for loose women.

42. Playing shirts and skins on the court.

43. Removing his shirt and seeing some skin off the court.

44. Working on making passes with the ball.

45. Working on making passes without the ball.

46. Kansas grads measure success one welfare check at a time.

47. Kansas requires that all entering freshmen be able to spell SAT, ACT, and IQ.

48. Coach Roy Williams thinks the final four is the last call for drinks.

49. The difference between a Kansas diploma and toilet paper is about $80,000 per sheet.

50. How does a Jayhawk spell the word *farm*?
E-I-E-I-O.

51. Kansas's football season opener is against Cal State Northridge, and it's all downhill from there.

52. The season opener will be broadcast on Comedy Central.

53. The captain of the Kansas cheerleading squad is the girl with the smallest fever blister.

54. For the past 50 years, Max Falkenstien has been the play-by-play broadcaster for the Jayhawk football team. Before that he was the public relations director for the Union during the Civil War.

55. Jayhawk cheerleaders are so ugly even Bill Clinton won't touch them.

56. When asked if he wanted to buy Easter Seals, baseball coach Roy Williams replied, "Are they good eatin'?"

57. Widespread septic tank leaks have given Memorial Stadium the brownest turf in the Big 12.

58. Most KU economics graduates leave school with only this 1 lasting piece of advice: Find a really dumb guy, ask if he's got 2 dimes for a nickel, and keep at it until you're rich.

59. Most KU graduates are so dull that they can't even entertain a doubt.

60. Sportscaster Max Falkenstien has gotten so old his thoughts have drifted from passion to pension.

61. How do you drown a KU sorority girl? Glue an American Express card to the bottom of a pool.

62. Jayhawk football players attribute their athletic abilities to "hard work, talent, and 12-ounce curls."

63. An academic All-American at KU is an athlete who can name 2 of his professors.

64. If you ask a Jayhawk what he hopes to be doing at 40, he'll likely respond, "graduating."

65. Jayhawk football players think that a book is something that is thrown at people.

66. The 10 toughest requirements for acceptance at Kansas University are: Knowing at least 5 of the letters in your last name.

67. Making at least a 14 on the ACT (unless you can dunk a basketball).

68. Correctly pointing to the United States on a globe. Getting the right hemisphere earns partial credit.

69. Eating 50 boiled eggs in an hour.

70. Correctly naming all the hosts of *The Tonight Show* since Johnny Carson.

71. You must be able to "Wave the Wheat."

72. Being able to correctly name Terry Allen's favorite pastime (hint: it isn't coaching football).

73. Correctly naming 1 state capital. Extra points for the capital of Kansas.

74. Confessing your favorite Spice Girl.

75. Looking interested even while you're asleep.

76. KU has 1 fewer football team than it needs.

77. KU students think safe sex means closing the car door.

78. In a shameless attempt to make ESPN's "Plays of the Week," KU's first baseman follows every routine putout with a curtsy.

79. The prettiest view of Lawrence is through a rearview mirror.

80. KU basketball players have led the conference in every category except hours spent in the library.

81. KU's "campus expansion" involved holding classes in abandoned boxcars.

82. The biggest difference between a Barbie doll and a KU cheerleader is that more plastic goes into putting together a KU cheerleader.

83. KU likes to brag that 80 percent of its players are from Kansas. (The rest of the country is too smart to go there.)

84. Athletic director Bob Frederick has 2 seats on press row–1 for himself and 1 for his ego.

85. KU's janitorial staff is composed entirely of alumni.

86. If you breed a Jayhawk with a groundhog you're guaranteed 6 more weeks of bad football.

87. *Gone with the Wind* describes KU's hopes of an NCAA championship during the third weekend in March.

88. Jayhawks are proof of reincarnation, because you can't get that dumb in just one lifetime.

89. You can get half off tuition at KU with every Happy Meal—and sometimes you get a diploma as a free prize.

90. Jayhawk basketball players are required to know how to spell ESPN before they graduate.

91. The top 10 reasons the Jayhawks can't win football games are: They keep forgetting that unlike soccer, in American football you can use your hands.

92. Kansas players are afraid of getting dirty.

93. Jayhawks are sensitive to the needs of the opposing team.

94. The opposing quarterback uses cool code names for plays instead of just yelling out the name of who he's going to throw to.

95. They compensate for not being bright by not being good athletes either.

96. It's hard to play football when you're worried whether your pet cow will win the 4-H fair this year.

97. The Jayhawk cheerleaders aren't allowed to play.

98. The opposing team's defense.

99. The opposing team's offense.

100. The other team always scores more points.

101. Bobby Randall is still trying to teach his players that a foul ball has nothing to do with its smell.

102. When he was asked to come up with a list of the 10 best games he had ever broadcast, Max Falkenstien said, "Huh?"

103. The hardest math class most Kansas football players take is "Subtraction: Addition's Tricky Friend."

104. The top 10 things happening the last time Kansas won the PAC 12 were: Harry Truman was President.

105. Tennessee Williams wrote "Cat on a Hot Tin Roof."

106. Americans broke the sound barrier.

107. Bell Laboratories invented the transistor.

108. Henry Ford died.

109. Al Capone died.

110. "All I Want for Christmas is My Two Front Teeth" was on the charts.

111. Peter Goldmark invented the LP.

112. Babe Ruth died.

113. Prince Charles was born.

114. The Jayhawk motto is "Have a cheerleader and a smile."

115. Most Jayhawks find that being a freshman can be the 6 hardest years of their lives.

116. To prove that the Jayhawk coeds are indeed creative, a poll was recently taken to determine their favorite sex positions. The top 5 choices were: the missionary position.

117. The missionary position.

118. The missionary position.

119. The missionary position.

120. The missionary position.

121. The Fabulous Sports Babe would be considered sexy on the Kansas campus.

122. KU students think that an instant camera must be stirred into boiling water.

123. KU professors rarely speak for more than 30 or 40 seconds at a time before becoming flustered and shouting, "Hey, ain't it break time already?"

124. What KU's campus desperately needs is a good detour.

125. Roy Williams is working on a book entitled *The 20 Biggest Games I've Choked In.*

126. KU basketball players have to climb chain link fences to see what's on the other side.

127. The best most KU wannabe's can get on their SATs is drool.

128. Scientists recently announced that at least 40% of the hole in the ozone layer is the direct result of hair spray used by KU cheerleaders.

129. Despite being on a totally landlocked campus, some KU students have chosen to flaunt their wealth by forming the Jayhawk Yacht Club.

130. Some KU coeds are so stuck-up that the bags under their eyes are by Gucci.

131. The KU med school never has to buy lab rats—they just look under the seats at Allen Fieldhouse.

132. If a train leaves Milwaukee at 2 p.m. going 40 mph and another train leaves Chicago at 3 p.m. going 50 mph, which train gets to KU first? The unlucky one.

133. The most popular course taken by KU athletes is "The College Classroom: A Simulation."

134. The second most popular class is "Cliff's Notes vs. Monarch Notes: 2 Views of the Classics."

135. Memorial Stadium is known for upholding tradition–too bad it's a losing one.

136. The 5 best things about the KU campus are: It's only 35 miles from Kansas City.

137. It's only 30 miles from Topeka.

138. It's only 37 miles from Overland Park.

139. It's only 81 miles from Manhattan.

140. It's only 161 miles from Wichita.

141. You can't spell the word *SUCK* without the letters *K* and *U*.

142. KU's most frequent alumni donations are returned diplomas.

143. Due to overwhelming player demand, next year's KU football jerseys will feature oversize lace collars.

144. KU's football program peaks in July.

145. Did you hear about the KU quarterback that tried to commit suicide? He didn't succeed because the bullet was intercepted.

146. KU grads study for 5 days to take a urine test and still fail.

147. KU basketball head coach Roy Williams has a hard time teaching players that dribbling is not the same thing as drooling.

148. The poll on which Kansas has finished first most often is the FBI most wanted.

149. What's red and blue, 100 yards long, and has 2 teeth? The front row at Memorial Stadium.

150. Coach Terry Allen once said, "The best thing about football is that it only takes four quarters to finish a fifth."

151. KU basketball recruits were getting paid before paying recruits was cool.

152. The fire at KU's library was a real tragedy because some of the books had yet to be colored.

153. The only thing KU and KSU students have in common is that both were accepted to KU.

154. Why is it always so hot at Memorial Stadium? Because there's not a fan in the place.

155. The KU football team is considering changing its name to the "Opossums" because they play dead at home and get killed on the road.

156. The Jayhawks used to have ice on their sidelines until the guy with the recipe graduated.

157. The only way to get a KU cheerleader in your room is to grease her hips and push.

158. KU is the only school where football players brag that they can bench press 5 times their own IQs.

159. A KU math professor once concluded that there are 3 kinds of people in this world: Those who can count and those who can't.

160. How many KU freshmen does it take to change a light bulb? None, it is a sophomore-level course.

161. A required course for KU coaches: "Your You-know-what from a Hole in the Ground."

162. When two or more KU players go out on a Saturday night, the designated driver usually winds up being a cop.

163. KU's graduation ceremony is traditionally followed by a caravan to K-State so grads can meet their new bosses.

164. KU's astronomy department claims that Mars is actually only 30 miles away—it's just really small.

165. A popular KU pickup line is "For a fat girl, you don't sweat much."

166. The usual response is "Thanks."

167. The Jayhawks dribble all over themselves, but that doesn't make them basketball players.

168. The best way to keep a Jayhawk out of your yard is to put up a goal post.

169. Terry Allen gets his team in the right frame of mind for every game by saying, "Don't worry. If we lose we can always blame the coaching."

170. If you drive slowly enough through the KU campus they'll likely give you a diploma.

171. The best form of birth control at KU is nudity.

172. Coach Terry Allen never drinks while driving because he's afraid he might spill his drink.

173. KU's soccer coach was recently heard yelling, "I've got it! We'll pass and shoot like in basketball, but no one will know because we'll wear shoes on our hands!"

174. Roy Williams has choked in so many big games that his assistants receive instruction in the Heimlich maneuver.

175. Some KU coeds walk with their noses turned so far up that you can actually see what they're thinking.

176. The 10 most popular classes with KU athletes are: "How to Hum: Lecture and Lab."

177. "U.S. History Since About an Hour Ago."

178. "The Science of Crayola."

179. "The Many Uses of Pork Fat."

180. "Our Alphabet and Why We Need It."

181. "Shiny Things and Why We Like Them."

182. "Recreation for Fun and Academic Credit."

183. "Nomadic Tribes of Sub-Saharan Africa that Are Really Just Lost."

184. "Republican Party Ethics."

185. "Words That Sound Funny."

186. A KU alum actually wrote a book on how to read.

187. The following books are required reading at the KU business school: *Line, Symbol, and Pie—Oh, Those Colorful Graphs!*

188. *Selecting the Clip-On Power Tie That's Right for You.*

189. *Elderly Employees Easier To Bully and Other Effective Hiring Strategies.*

190. *Funny-Looking People on Foreign Money: A History.*

191. *Make Big $$$ Selling Your Unused Prescriptions.*

192. Ever since the news broke about Mad Cow Disease, nobody has kissed a KU cheerleader.

193. Lawrence may not be the end of the world, but you sure can see it from there.

194. Coach Terry Allen never bores anybody by saying too much—he can do it by saying very little.

195. A Jayhawk coed sold her computer because it missed a period and she thought it was pregnant.

196. Many KU students minimize their food budgets by scheduling classes around Happy Hour.

197. The top 10 ways you know it's finals time at KU: College administration is considering treating the campus water supply with Prozac.

198. Workers at campus restaurants have been issued mace for "low on caffeinated beverages" emergencies.

199. Local stores are sold out of all chocolate and caffeine products.

200. A job at Burger King looks pretty good compared to completing your education.

201. Certain professors have hired bodyguards.

202. Ticket scalpers are selling empty spaces in the computer labs.

203. The local psychic hotline branches out into essay questions and term papers.

204. The Hell's Angels plan their trip around the college out of fear of getting into a brawl.

205. Football players are trying to find their class schedules.

206. Disgruntled postal employees run in fear from students.

207. Jayhawk football practice is often disrupted for 45 minutes at a time by mirthful linebackers playing "pull my finger."

208. When chancellor Robert E. Hemenway asked his doctor for a way to cure his insomnia, his doctor replied, "Try listening to yourself talk."

209. Former coach Larry Brown once said that his fondest memory of KU was the day he left.

210. Some KU sorority girls can't tell it's raining until water gets in their noses.

211. The only good thing to come out of Lawrence is I-70.

212. Substitute professors at KU are often just salesmen attempting to unload overpriced cleaning products on the student body.

213. One KU student was such a compulsive gambler that, after losing a bet on a horse race, he went double-or-nothing on the instant replay.

214. Before receiving their diplomas, KU players must show proof-of-purchase slips for at least 2 textbooks.

215. When a KU athlete won a silver medal in Atlanta he was so proud that he had it bronzed.

216. The top 10 things taught to incoming freshmen at KU orientation: Earn extra cash by parlaying chemistry knowledge into lucrative "home pharmaceuticals" business.

217. If an 8:00 A.M. class is required for your major, change your major.

218. Boring lecture? Start a wave!

219. College-level algebra: 5 returnable bottles = 1 delicious Ramen Noodle dinner.

220. "I Phelta Thi" is not a real fraternity, except at KU.

221. No one complains when you puke in a dumpster.

222. Clever margin manipulation can turn a 4-page outline into a 100-page senior essay.

223. Football games were never meant to be observed by sober people.

224. Don't think of it as sleeping with your professor—think of it as acing biology.

225. In a pinch, milk can be used as a beer substitute in your breakfast cereal.

226. Jayhawks are proof positive that you should never under-estimate the power of stupid people in large groups.

227. Six words guaranteed to break the heart of a KU cheerleader are "Sorry, honey, we're out of bacon."

228. KU students think that lowfat milk comes from skinny cows.

229. Will Rogers never met Roy Williams.

230. Jayhawk football players spend 20 minutes at a time staring at orange juice cans that say "concentrate."

231. Someone needs to tell the head of KU's medical school that Dr. Pepper isn't really medicine.

232. The top 10 reasons this year's incoming freshmen chose to attend Kansas are: Kansas-State University was full.

233. The University of Oklahoma was too far away.

234. The University of Missouri was too expensive.

235. They wanted to attend a school that didn't have a successful football program.

236. Their parents didn't want them to be distracted by having to miss class to go to the Final Four.

237. They wanted to go to a school where they wouldn't be intimidated by good-looking students.

238. They wanted to go to a school where they wouldn't be intimidated by smart students.

239. They wanted to attend a school where the football coach was *not* a role model.

240. In a recent poll, 70 percent of KU football players said rain came from Canada.

241. Fourth-quarter huddles often involve the quarterback saying, "No, I haven't got any ideas either, but I would like to take this opportunity to pass out some Binaca."

242. KU cheerleaders are tested weekly for make-up poisoning.

243. First prize in a recent radio giveaway was a pair of KU football tickets. Second prize was 2 pairs.

244. KU is proof that things don't always improve with age.

245. The KU football team's defense often avoids physical contact with the other team in the second half on the grounds that "those guys are all messy and sweaty."

246. Usually the biggest bone of contention when KU grads divorce is who gets to keep the trailer.

247. Students at KU believe that Diet Coke will help them lose weight and get high at the same time.

248. A popular saying at K-State is "A tie is like kissing a KU girl."

249. Most KU Law School graduates still think "Roe vs. Wade" is a decision to be made before crossing a creek.

250. Most Jayhawk players say the reason they don't want to play for the Canadian Football League is that they don't enjoy traveling overseas.

251. You can tell when a Jayhawk has been using your computer because there's white-out on the screen.

252. The fact that Memorial Stadium holds 50,000 just shows how little there is to do in Lawrence.

253. If KU's linebackers were any slower, they'd be in reverse.

254. Coach Roy Williams's favorite kind of party is whine and cheese.

255. The *University Daily Kansan* never prints the odds on the Jayhawk football team beating Nebraska because their keyboard doesn't have the infinity sign.

256. The median IQ of Lawrence doubles every time the Jayhawk football team plays an away game.

257. If KU students seem upset at graduation, it's because they realize they'll soon have to learn to spell the name of another city.

258. What do KU girls make for dinner? Reservations.

259. One KU cheerleader donated her body to science before she was through using it.

260. The longest rush from scrimmage last year by a KU running back was to the sideline for an "ouchless" Band-Aid.

261. Coach Roy Williams's ego is so huge that he bows when it thunders.

262. Coach Roy Williams often contradicts himself—and he's usually right.

263. Coach Terry Allen is so cheap that he told his children Christmas is on December 28 so he could take advantage of the sales.

264. Chancellor Robert E. Hemenway is such a humanitarian that he donated $10,000 to the family of the Unknown Soldier.

265. Mug shots are becoming popular alternatives for graduation photos in the KU yearbook.

266. A favorite pickup line of KU football players is "Hey, didn't we almost flunk out together?"

267. KU fans think that a honeymoon is when lovers bare their buttocks towards a public building.

268. Coach Roy Williams never lets facts interfere with his opinions.

269. KU has started a javelin retrieval team.

270. KU's pacifist defensive coordinator has taught his players that before hitting anyone, they should take a deep breath, count to 10, and try to cool off.

271. O. J. Simpson should have fled to Lawrence—nobody would think to look for a football player there.

272. The only thing worse than a KU fan is 2 KU fans.

273. Jayhawk basketball players like to disrupt games by sucking the air out of the ball to get a quick buzz.

274. Somehow tornadoes and KU grads always wind up in trailer parks.

275. Chancellor Robert E. Hemenway defends his university by saying, "Unlike *some* schools I could name, KU's professors won't be skipping classes to accept any of those fancy Nobel prizes anytime soon."

276. Most KU grads believe that non-dairy creamer comes from dehydrated cows.

277. The Jayhawk mascot is tested for distemper twice a month.

278. The KU coaching staff had to start holding separate Wives' Day and Girlfriends' Day because some guys were bringing both.

279. KU is the Kmart of education.

280. The KU weight room features La-Z-Boy products.

281. It's a good thing KU fans don't have to pass an IQ test to qualify for season tickets.

282. Before hiring a new assistant coach, Roy Williams told athletic director Bob Frederick, "We don't need to get rid of any coaches, we just need a way to get rid of the alumni."

283. KU holds the patent on the inflatable dart board.

284. The biggest difference between Jayhawks fans and puppies is that puppies usually stop whining when they grow up.

285. Despite KU's desperate petitioning, the Big 8 is not going to be the first conference in the NCAA to convert to the Nerf football.

286. KU cheerleaders have bubbles in their think tanks.

287. One KU recruit got his red BMW the hard way—he bought it.

288. The food at some KU restaurants is so bad that the only card they take is Blue Cross.

289. Most KU players' lists of accomplishments read like rap sheets.

290. KU athletic trainers have been known to treat injured athletes with nothing but some Nair and a pair of pliers.

291. KU's greatest academic achievement was a brochure explaining the correct way to set VCR locks.

292. KU cheerleaders don't like to lie out in the sun because the heat might melt their plastic surgery.

293. Most KU grads are so dull that they make the Amish look like Hell's Angels.

294. If it weren't for the simple pleasures of origami, KU diplomas would be almost completely useless.

295. KU's most popular campus organization is the Hair Club for Men.

296. Roy Williams is such an egotist that his head has its own zip code.

297. Most KU football players believe that sentences end in an appeal.

298. It's easy to tell when finals are approaching at KU—the basketball players start buying their books.

299. If Roy Williams concentrated as much on the game as he does on his wardrobe, the Jayhawks might win another championship.

300. If Roy Williams were the captain of the *Titanic*, he'd have said, "We're just stopping for ice."

301. KU fans have a love-hate relationship with Nebraska coach Frank Solich. They'd love for him to retire because they hate losing to him every year.

302. KU students think they're getting a "higher education" just because KU is on a hill.

303. What do you do if a KU fan throws a hand grenade at you? Pull the pin and throw it back.